Editorial Project Manager
Mara Ellen Guckian

Illustrator
Vanessa Countryman

Cover Artist
Kevin Barnes

Editor In Chief
Ina Massler Levin, M.A.

Creative Director
Karen J. Goldfluss, M.S. Ed.

Art Production Manager
Kevin Barnes

Art Coordinator
Renée Christine Yates

Imaging
Craig Gunnell
Nathan P. Rivera

Publisher

Mary D. Smith, M.S. Ed.

D0127324

Written and Compiled by
Debbie Kahnen Lytle,
Mara Ellen Guckian, and Marian Weber

Teacher Created Resources, Inc.
6421 Industry Way
Westminster, CA 92683
www.teachercreated.com

ISBN: 978-1-4206-5140-9

©2008 Teacher Created Resources, Inc.

Reprinted, 2013

Made in U.S.A.

Teacher Created Resources

Table of Contents

Introduction

Why write a book about projects using hands and feet? Simple—it is fun and the materials needed are readily available. The projects cover a wide range of curricular areas and holidays. These suggested activities are not simply "art projects" but will encourage creativity while developing students' fine motor skills through cutting, tracing and assembling.

The collection of songs and finger plays in the beginning of the book will get younger students' attention. Each song includes movements that focus on developing fine motor skills. Additionally, the tips for drawing, cutting, and tracing should prove useful for students not yet as skilled as they need to be. Older students may be ready to start right in tracing their hands, shoeprints or footprints and assembling a variety of fun projects.

The activities provided in this book are organized by month. Some of the ideas revolve around holiday decorations while others are seasonal or pertain to typical topics of interest in classrooms. A variety of suggestions for displaying the finished projects are given. Some projects lend themselves to bulletin boards, others to door or window decorations. Still others can be hung from the ceilings. Many of the projects can be displayed as is or can be used as backdrops to highlight student writing or other work.

As educators, you will find many ways to incorporate academics pertinent to your curriculum into these projects. Students should enjoy the personalized touch that each of their prints add to the activities. Have fun!

Songs for Hands and Feet

My Hands
(Traditional)

My hands upon my head I place,
On my shoulders,
On my face.
Then I hold them way up high,
Let my fingers fly, fly, fly.
Clap, clap, clap,
And a one, two, three!
See how quiet they can be.

Movements: Encourage students to listen to the song a few times. Do they hear any words that rhyme? What actions might they do while singing? Talk about the suggested actions, and then ask them to add the actions as they sing.

Head, Shoulders, Knees and Toes
(Traditional)

Head, shoulders, knees and toes,
knees and toes,
Head, shoulders, knees and toes,
Knees and toes,
Eyes and ears and mouth and nose,
Head, shoulders, knees and toes, knees and toes.

Movements: This song is a great one to sing when students have lots of energy. Have students stand with their hands on their heads to begin. Continue singing, placing both hands on the body parts as they are mentioned. Once students are familiar with the song, add additional body parts. Another variation might be to adjust the speed of the song. Try it very slowly and build up to a rapid rendition. Try singing it loud or in a whisper.

Songs for Hands and Feet *(cont.)*

I Can
(Sing to the tune of "The Wheels on the Bus.")

I can make my hands go clap, clap, clap,
Clap, clap, clap,
Clap, clap, clap.
I can make my hands go clap, clap, clap,
They're a part of me.
I can make my feet go stomp, stomp, stomp,
Stomp, stomp, stomp,
Stomp, stomp, stomp.
I can make my feet go stomp, stomp, stomp,
They're a part of me.

Movements: Sing the song for students a few times, demonstrating the actions. As soon as students are comfortable with the lyrics, ask for suggestions to add to the song. Additional lines might include the following:

| …eyes go blink | …arms go flap | …head go nod |
| …hips go wiggle | …legs go jump | …tongue go in and out |

Two Little Feet
(Traditional)

Two little hands go clap, clap, clap.
Two little feet go tap, tap, tap.
One little body leaps up from the chair.
Two little arms go up in the air.

Two little hands go thump, thump, thump.
Two little feet go jump, jump, jump.
One little body goes round and round,
and one little student sits quietly down.

Movements: Sing the song for students a few times, demonstrating the actions suggested. Begin this song seated in chairs and encourage students to act out the verses in a vigorous manner, finishing the song by again sitting quietly.

Songs for Hands and Feet *(cont.)*

Where Is Thumbkin?
(Traditional)

Where is Thumbkin?
Where is Thumbkin?
Here I am.
Here I am!
How are you today, sir?
Very well, I thank you.
Run a-way, run a-way.

Where is Pointer?
Where is Tall Man?
Where is Ring Man?
Where is Pinkie?

Movements: Talk about the different names for the thumb and fingers. Share the names that will be used in this song (See diagram below.).

Have students begin with both hands behind their backs. On the first phrase, "Here I am," instruct students to hold up the thumbs of one hand. If appropriate, specify the right or left hand. Hold up the thumb on the other hand for the second "Here I am" phrase. Continue holding up different fingers while singing. After Thumbkin, call for Pointer, Tall Man, Ring Man, and Pinkie.

Songs for Hands and Feet (cont.)

Ten Little Fingers
(Traditional)

I have ten little fingers,
And they all belong to me.
I can make them do things,
Would you like to see?

I can shut them up tight,
Or open them up wide.
I can put them all together,
Or I can make them hide!

I can make them jump high,
Or wiggle them down low,
I can fold them quietly,
And hold them just so!

Movements: This little song is a great one for getting the wiggles out before settling down for activities, rest time, quiet reading, etc.

If You're Happy
(Traditional)

If you're happy and you know it,
Clap your hands.
If you're happy and you know it,
Clap your hands.
If you're happy and you know it,
Then your face will surely show it.
If you're happy and you know it, clap your hands!

Movements: Choose other students to suggest and model additional sounds or motions. Possible variations might include:

If you're happy and you know it, *stamp your feet… tickle your tummy… wave hello!*

Songs for Hands and Feet *(cont.)*

Clap, Clap, Clap Your Hands
(Sing to the tune "Row, Row, Row Your Boat.")

Clap, clap, clap your hands,
Clap your hands together.
Clap, clap, clap your hands,
In all kinds of weather.

Stretch, stretch, stretch your arms,
Stretch your arms together.
Stretch, stretch, stretch your arms,
In all kinds of weather.

Reach, reach, reach your arms,
Reach your arms together.
Reach, reach, reach up high,
In all kinds of weather.

Tap, tap, tap your toes,
Tap your toes together.
Tap, tap, tap your toes,
In all kinds of weather.

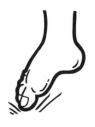

Stamp, stamp, stamp your feet,
Stamp your feet together.
Stamp, stamp, stamp your feet,
In all kinds of weather.

Additional lines:
Nod, nod, nod your heads...
Come, let's all sit down...

Movements: Hum the song first to see if students recognize the melody. Then share the words and invite students to join in as soon as they feel comfortable.

Skills Development

Holding a Writing Implement

Holding a writing implement correctly takes practice. Some schools of thought suggest using a fat crayon first since the crayon needs to be pressed onto the paper to create lines or color. Others believe that a large marker (felt pen) is a better writing implement to start with since it flows smoothly on the paper. Either way, the first three fingers are the most important when learning to write. Have the student practice by tapping the middle finger against the thumb. Have the student switch back and forth between tapping his or her middle finger and thumb to tapping his or her pointer finger and thumb. While the student has the middle finger tapped against the thumb, slide the crayon in to rest above the thumb. The pointer finger does the guiding. Write in the air before you initiate writing on paper. Suggest large circles and get progressively smaller. Try different shapes or types of lines, including zigzag lines and wavy ones. Whenever possible, encourage young writers to use thicker writing implements until their fine motor skills are more developed.

Tracing Tips

Most of us do not remember the first time we tried to trace something. It seems like such a simple thing to do, but it does take a certain amount of practice and fine motor skill development. Tracing requires time and practice to perfect.

To trace, one must hold an object steady with one hand while maneuvering around it with the other hand. For some students, it helps to put a little piece of rolled-up tape on the under side of the paper while tracing to prevent the paper from moving. The hand used to write holds the pencil or crayon and traces around the object. The other hand should be used to hold the item steady while it is being traced. If it still sounds simple, try doing it yourself but hold the pencil in the opposite hand that you usually use. You should notice a certain awkwardness when trying to cross over the hand holding the item being traced.

Before trying to trace an item on paper, have students trace over shapes drawn on the paper. They can start tracing with their fingers and gradually move to using writing implements. Get them accustomed to following lines instead of drawing freely. Many students like to trace over the letters in their names as well.

Provide simple shapes for those new to tracing. Large flat plates work well initially. They are heavy, can fit the student's whole "holding hand," and stay in place easily. As skills improve, cut shapes from heavy cardboard or the colorful foam sheets sold in craft stores. Provide seasonal shapes for added interest. When appropriate, introduce hand tracing. Encourage students to spread their fingers wide when tracing their own hands.

Tracing Practice

Tracing Practice *(cont.)*

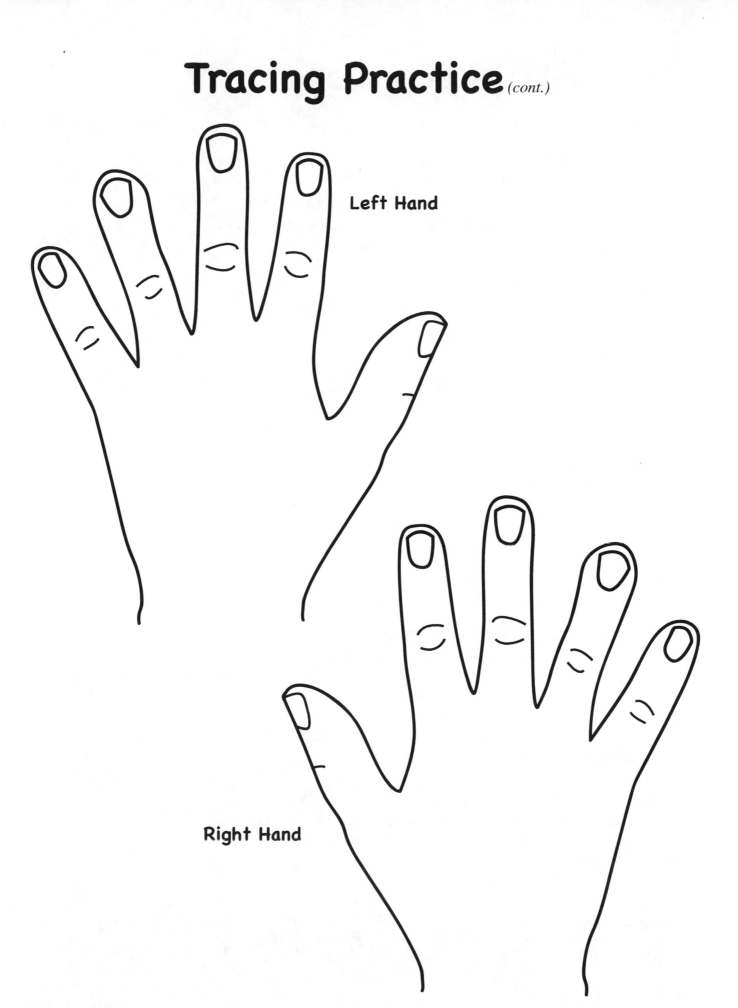

Left Hand

Right Hand

Skills Development *(cont.)*

Using Scissors

At first glance, cutting with scissors seems pretty simple, but put scissors in the hands of a young student, and the challenges become quite clear. A student's ability to cut accurately depends on his or her muscle development. Many students need to strengthen their hand muscles before attempting to cut paper.

Developing hand muscles (fine motor skills) can be done with simple finger plays, especially those requiring the student to open and close his or her fingers. Other classroom activities that can help develop fine motor skills include:

- squeezing clay
- wringing out wet sponges
- using plastic eyedroppers to drip colored water into ice cube trays or onto coffee filters
- picking up items with tongs
- using clothespins and tweezers

What type of scissors should be used?

Purchase scissors that can be used in either the left or the right hand. Always buy "safety" scissors with rounded tips to prevent accidents. Plastic or rubber grips are a great help too.

Scissors Safety

Discuss safety rules with students before handing out scissors. Review the rules often.

1. When carrying the scissors, hold them like a bunch of flowers. Hold the stems (shaft) with the flowers (handles) showing on the top.
2. Always walk when carrying scissors, never run.
3. Only cut things you have permission to cut.
4. Hand scissors to someone with the holes facing the person, not the blades.

How should the scissors be held?

Teaching a student how to hold the scissors properly can minimize many of the frustrations that revolve around cutting. First, show the student how you hold a pair of adult-sized scissors. Next, help the student position his or her hand on a pair of student-sized scissors. The thumb goes in the smaller of the two holes. The next two or three fingers go in the larger hole. After the fingers are placed correctly in the scissors' handles, explain that it is important to keep the thumb up.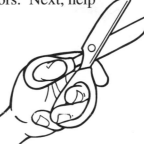

Teacher Note: Most students show some hand dominance at about the age of three, but don't show a real preference until they reach kindergarten. Allow the student to choose which hand he or she prefers when holding a pair of scissors. It may change from one hand to the other, even during a single cutting project.

Cutting Practice

For many students, this will be a review, but for some the tips may help a great deal. Ask each student to move his or her thumb and fingers so that the scissor blades separate. Open and close the blades numerous times. Point out that the open blades form a "V" that looks like a mouth chomping. Demonstrate how to place the paper to be cut all the way to the V (place where the blades meet) and squeeze up and down, using the handles. Have the student pretend to chomp as he or she moves the blades. Allow the students to experience cutting at their own pace.

Beginner

Once a student is comfortable opening and closing the blades of the scissors, provide small strips of tagboard, paint sample strips or junk mail to cut up. Try to use paper that is a bit stiffer than drawing paper. It is easier to hold while cutting. Strips that only require one or two snips to cut through like paint samples are also good. They allow students to feel successful with minimal effort.

Intermediate

Intermediate cutters can continue practicing their skills by cutting larger pieces of paper or other paper items. Keep a plastic tub or shoebox filled with materials to be cut on hand. To maintain interest, change the materials from time to time. Some suggested materials include:

- cards
- catalogs
- construction paper
- drinking straws
- foil
- junk mail

- newspapers
- old greeting cards
- play dough
- sandpaper
- wallpaper
- wax paper

Advanced

Advanced cutters are ready for cutting out more intricate shapes. Provide these students with opportunities to practice cutting out both large and small shapes. The shapes should be increasingly more complex with more curves and corners. Soon, they will be ready to try cutting out tracings of their own hands and feet!

Seasonal Tree

Materials

- pencils
- safety scissors
- red, yellow, light brown, and orange construction paper
- brown wrapping paper or paper bags
- Tree Trunk patterns (pages 15 and 16), enlarged
- *optional*: tape

Procedure

1. Have students take turns tracing their hands onto fall-colored construction paper. Put a little piece of rolled-up tape on the under side of the construction paper while tracing. This helps prevent the paper from moving. Remind students to keep the hand that is on the paper still and use their other hand to move the pencil.

2. When students have finished tracing their hands, provide scissors for them to cut out the tracings.

3. Encourage students to make more than one leaf (hand). This activity can be an ongoing one during the fall.

Display Suggestion

Create a class tree to be used for the entire school term.

1. Enlarge the tree trunk patterns and trace or draw them on brown paper to fit the display area or bulletin board. If appropriate, ask students to help.

2. Have students help crumple up the brown paper trunk and smooth it out again. The crumpling will create ridges similar to tree bark. Additional brown crayon lines can be added from top to bottom.

3. Attach the tree trunk to the display area.

4. Encourage students to point to where they would like their hand-shaped leaves to be placed on the tree. Use directional words (spatial concepts) like *above*, *beside*, *near*, and *below*.

Tree Trunk Top

Directions: To create the top of the tree, place this pattern on the crease of a folded piece of brown paper and trace it. Cut out the pattern and unfold it to create the top half of a tree.

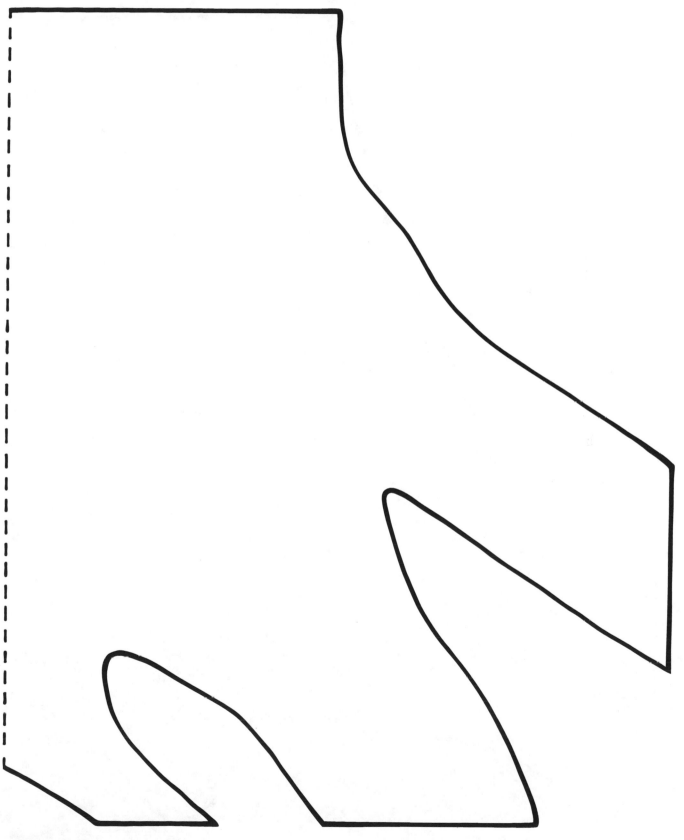

Tree Trunk Base

Directions: To create the base of the tree, place this pattern on the crease of a folded piece of brown paper and trace it. Cut out the pattern and unfold it to create the lower half of a tree.

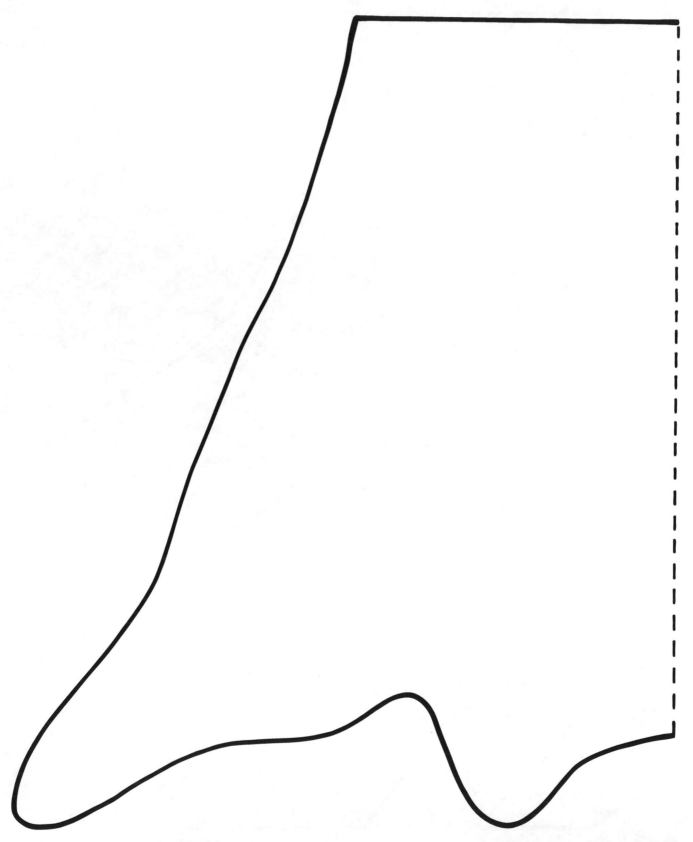

Trees for All Seasons

Materials

- brown tempera paint
- cookie sheet with sides
- light blue construction paper
- seasonal tree patterns (pages 18–19)
- newspaper
- hand soap, water, and towels
- painting smocks
- crayons or markers

Teacher Notes

1. This project (arm trees) can be done four separate times during the year to celebrate the changing seasons. If necessary, all four trees can be made at the same time, dried, and filed away for later use.

2. Adult assistance is suggested when making the arm/hand prints. Students who will be painting should be advised to wear messy clothes or to cover up with smocks or old shirts.

Alternative: If painting is not an option, students can trace their hands and arms on brown paper instead. Tracings can be cut out individually, or stacks of paper can be added and cut with assistance.

Preparation

1. Prepare an area for painting and establish a cleanup area close by.

2. Pour a thin layer of brown paint in the cookie sheet and place the tray on newspaper.

Procedure

1. Explain to students that they will be using their hands and arms to create trees. Their arms, from elbow to wrist, will form the tree's trunk, and their hands, with fingers spread, will be the branches.

2. Place the student's arm, bent at the elbow, in the tray of paint.

3. Have the student spread his or her fingers. Lay the arm, with fingers spread, on a piece of light blue construction paper and press gently (Repeat the process if necessary for additional copies.).

4. Carefully lift the arm straight up off the paper and have student wash his or her arm and hand.

5. Label the student's page and set it aside to dry.

6. Decorate the tree using the patterns and markers or crayons to suit the season.

Display Suggestions

There are many possibilities for displaying these works of art. You may wish to label each student's tree page and display them on a bulletin board for the entire season. Then they can be removed and saved in portfolios until the end of the school year. Another option would be to display subsequent seasons on top of the completed ones. The four can be bound together at the end of the school term creating a book.

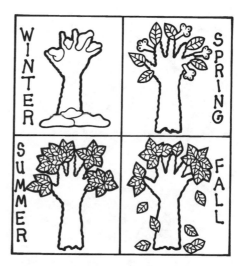

Trees for All Seasons *(cont.)*

Seasonal Tree Patterns

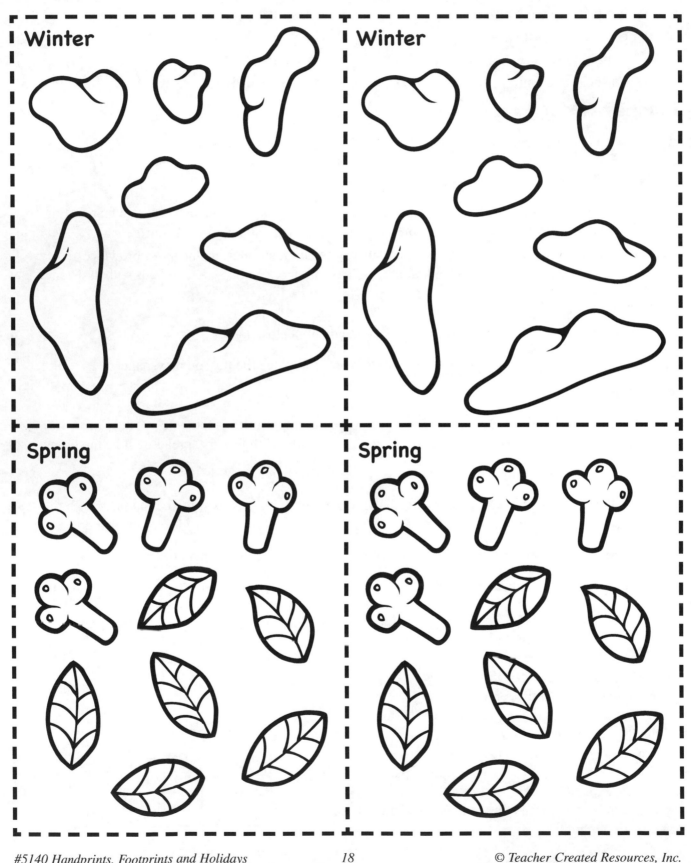

Winter

Winter

Spring

Spring

Trees for All Seasons *(cont.)*

Seasonal Tree Patterns *(cont.)*

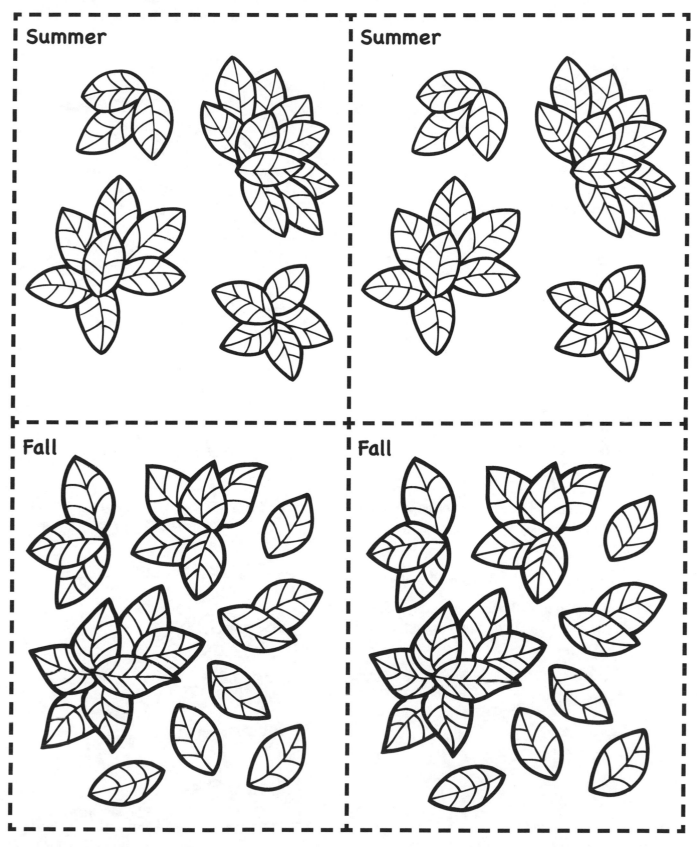

Germs

For many of us, September is the start of the school year and the beginning of cold season. Here is a little project to introduce a discussion on preventing the spread of germs. Discuss the many ways to prevent the spread of germs before this activity. You may wish to create a list on chart paper to post in the classroom.

Here are a few ideas to get you started:

Wash hands with soap and water before eating.
Wash hands with soap and water after using the restroom.
Use a tissue to blow your nose.
Cover your nose and mouth with your elbow, not your hands, when sneezing.

Germs Make Me Sick!

Materials

- Germs Make Me Sick! worksheet (page 21)
- box of tissue
- crayons or markers
- glue or a stapler
- skin-toned construction paper
- scissors

Procedure

1. Instruct students to color the face outlines to look like themselves.

2. Fold a piece of paper in half so that a hand will fit on it.

3. Have each student trace his or her hand with his or her wrist resting on the fold. You may wish to specify which hand to reinforce—*left* or *right*.

4. Have each student cut out his or her hands.

5. Ask students to glue the base (wrist) of each hand to one of the **Xs**. Explain that they want the hands to cover the nose.

6. Glue a tissue to the inside of one of the hands to make it look as if the nose is being blown.

Germs Make Me Sick!

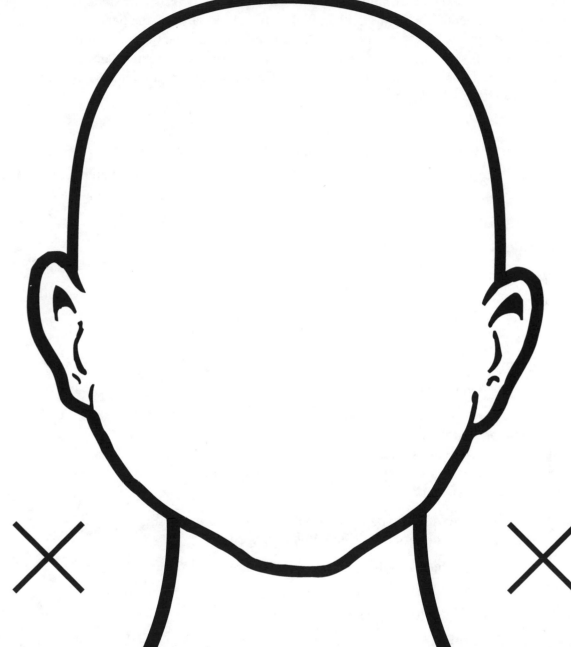

Procedure

1. Color the face to look like you.

2. Trace your hands .

3. Cut them out, and glue the bases (wrists) of them to the **Xs**.

4. Glue a tissue to the inside of the hand to cover your mouth and nose.

5. This is how to keep your germs to yourself!

Ghostly Visitors

There are two ways to approach creating these cute ghosts. If the handprints are done first on large pieces of paper, older students can draw (freehand) ghostly outlines around the hands and add faces. Or, the pattern provided on pages 23–24 can be assembled, and copies can be made for younger students to use. Do not worry which side students add their handprints to or which direction the paper is going; the reversed or sideways patterns will make the completed display look more unique. After all, do we really know what a ghost's shape is?

Materials

- white butcher paper or ghost patterns (page 23–24)
- background paper for bulletin board
- black or gray tempera paint
- cookie sheets with sides
- black markers
- newspaper
- hand soap, water, and towels
- painting smocks
- *optional:* border trim

Preparation

1. Prepare an area for painting and establish a cleanup area close by.

2. Pour a thin layer of paint in the cookie tray and place the tray on newspaper.

Procedure

1. Give each student a ghost pattern or large piece of white paper.

2. Explain that they will be adding faces and handprints to their ghostly shapes and that the idea is for each ghost to look different. There is no right or wrong way to shape the ghost or use the pattern. Have each student write his or her name on the back of his or her ghost shape.

3. Ask students to draw faces where they wish on the ghost shape. They can place the paper horizontally, vertically, or diagonally.

4. Take turns dipping both hands in the paint tray and making left and right handprints on the ghost.

5. Lay the finished ghosts flat to dry so the handprints do not run.

6. If appropriate, allow time for students to trim ghosts to enhance shapes.

Display Suggestions

- Attach background paper and border trim to the display area. Arrange the ghosts on the bulletin board. If room allows, use the ghosts as backgrounds to feature student work. Add an appropriate title to the display area.

- Ghosts can be added to the surrounding walls and suspended from the ceiling.

Ghost Pattern A

Use with pattern on page 24.

Ghost Pattern B

Use with pattern on page 23.

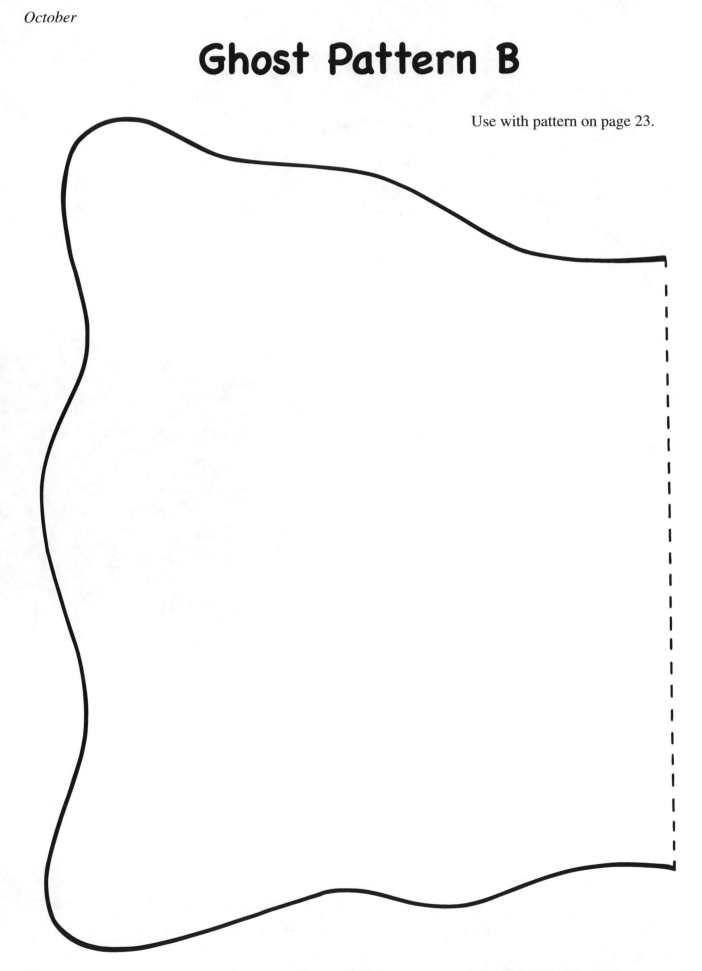

Spiders on a Web

Materials

- black construction paper
- black or gray butcher paper
- white crayons
- wiggly eyes or hole punch circles for eyes
- safety scissors
- glue sticks
- *optional:* yarn for web—consider sparkly silver, gray, white or orange

Procedure

1. Fold the black construction paper in half, horizontally.

2. Have students use white crayons to trace their hands on the black paper. Explain that they will be creating spider legs with their fingers. The base of their palms should be placed off the folded edge (See diagram.). The fingers need to be spread as wide as possible. Thumbs should be curled in but not on the paper. This will create a more rounded shape for the spider legs.

3. Carefully cut out the completed tracing and unfold the paper to view the spider.

4. Demonstrate for the students how to slightly bend the legs to look more spider-like.

5. Give each student a glue stick and some eyes. Share with students that most spiders have eight eyes arranged in a circular fashion. Model for students how to glue the eyes on top of the spider.

Display Suggestion

Make a spider web scene on a bulletin board or display area.

1. Begin by covering the background with black butcher paper.

2. Make the web by drawing on the background paper with white chalk, crayon, or paint. The web can also be made with white yarn. Start the web at the center of the background. Begin by making spokes, or straight lines, moving outward from the center point.

3. After you have put in the spokes, return to the center to create the spiral part of the web. Start small and work your way around to the outer edge of the web.

4. Attach the hand-shaped spiders to the bulletin board. Encourage the students to point to where they want their spiders to be placed.

5. Add an appropriate title to the display.

Bats

Materials

- black construction paper
- white crayons
- safety scissors
- *optional*: wiggly eyes, glitter, and silver or orange bulletin board paper

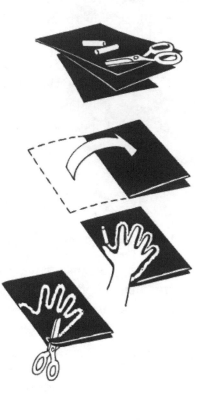

Procedure

1. Fold the black paper in half, lengthwise.

2. Place one hand flat on the paper with the edge of the thumb along the fold. Mention to students that they will be tracing along one side of the thumb and that the other side will rest on the fold line.

3. Trace along the hand with the white crayon.

4. Cut around the white outline of the hand.

5. Unfold the paper.

6. Add features to the bat with the white crayon or other materials.

Display Suggestions

- Make bat wreaths by placing several bat cutouts in a circle and adding orange bows for decorations. If appropriate, create a sign or card saying "Happy Halloween." Sprinkle the wreaths with silver or black glitter.

- Hang each student's completed bat from the ceiling. Add silver stars and a moon to create a night-sky effect.

- Create a bulletin board display. Use silver or orange paper as a background. Bats can be placed all over the board as if flying in a night sky, or they can be used to highlight a selection of the student's work.

Class Turkey

This group project can make a wonderful door display or room decoration. Pair students to work on creating a multitude of different colored feathers.

Materials

- turkey body patterns (page 28–29)
- red, orange, yellow, light and dark brown construction paper
- safety scissors
- glue sticks

Preparation

1. Enlarge the turkey body to fit the display area.

2. Trace the body onto light brown construction paper and cut it out.

3. Add a red head and wattle to the turkey.

4. Add an orange beak and orange or yellow feet.

5 Cut the colored construction paper sheets in half.

Procedure

1. Ask students what is missing on the turkey body. Guide them toward the answer of *feathers* and explain that their handprints will be the feathers.

2. Have students pair up and choose from the selection of construction paper to make feathers.

3. Have paired students take turns tracing around each other's spread hands on construction paper.

Display Suggestion

Create a door decoration or wall display.

Fan out the multi-colored construction paper hands on the back of the turkey to represent the turkey's tail feathers. If appropriate, label the turkey with the words "Happy Thanksgiving."

Class Turkey *(cont.)*

Turkey Patterns

head/neck

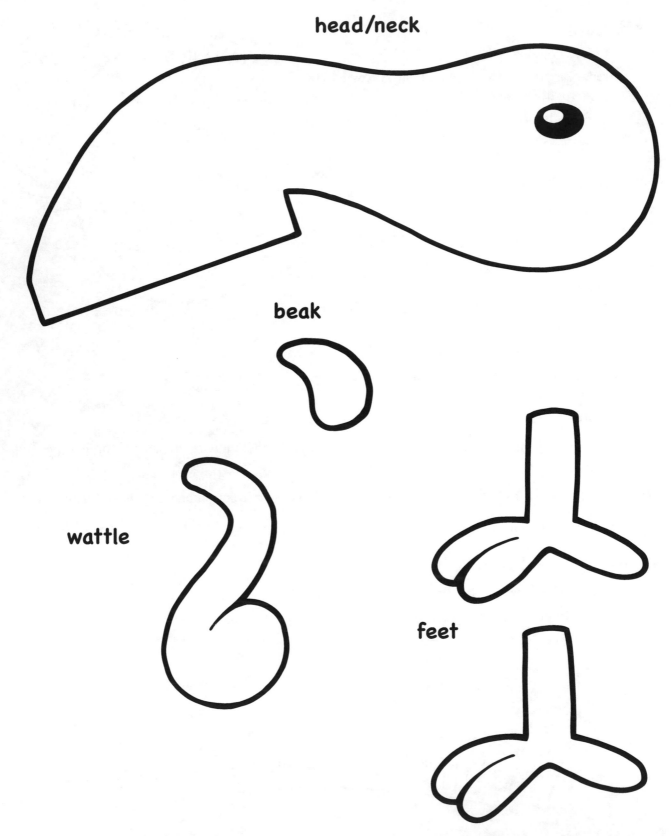

beak

wattle

feet

28

Class Turkey *(cont.)*

body with wing

Turkeys, Turkeys Everywhere

Materials

- colored feathers (can be found in craft shops and art supply stores)
- light or medium brown construction paper
- glue sticks   •   crayons   •   pencils   •   safety scissors

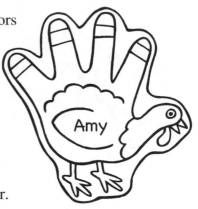

Procedure

1. Have students spread the fingers on one hand wide and trace it onto light brown construction paper (The lighter brown will make it easier to see the tracing line.).

2. Cut out the hand tracing. The thumb will become the head of the turkey, and the fingers will become the feathers.

3. Glue the brown hand shapes to a piece of light blue construction paper.

4. Draw an eye and add a red wattle (oval) and a beak (2 triangles) at the tip of the turkey's head (thumb). Don't forget to label each turkey with the student's name.

5. Add two turkey legs under the palm of the body of the turkey (hand).

6. Glue real or purchased feathers to the fingers to represent tail feathers.

7. Have each student cut around the area of his or her turkey.

Display Suggestion
Materials

- green or brown bulletin board paper
- *optional*: birdseed or cornmeal
- light blue bulletin board paper
- *optional:* tree, barn, fences, etc.

Procedure

1. Create a barnyard scene. Use light blue and light brown or green paper to create the sky and ground.

2. Consider gluing birdseed or cornmeal here and there on the brown paper before hanging it up. This could serve as food for the turkeys scratching about the yard.

3. Add a barn, fences, etc. to the scene. Title it *Turkeys, Turkeys Everywhere.*

4. Ask students to choose where they would like their cut-out turkeys to be placed in the barnyard.

Holiday Wreath

Materials

- green construction paper
- red tissue paper or pom poms
- large red bow
- pencils and markers
- safety scissors

Procedure

1. Have students trace their hands on green construction paper.

2. Provide scissors for each of them to cut out the hands they traced.

3. Add a few red paper berries to each hand pattern. To do this, have students use pom poms or tear small pieces of red tissue paper. Crumple the tissue paper into balls and glue them to the palm part of the hands.

Teacher's Note: Encourage students to make several hand shapes so there are enough hands to form a large, full wreath.

Alternative: Have students dip their hands in green tempera paint to create handprints.

Display Suggestion

Create a bulletin board or door decoration with this wreath. Personalize it to suit classroom needs and seasonal themes.

1. Attach the hand shapes in a circular, overlapping pattern onto a bulletin board or large piece of butcher paper. Some of the fingers should point to the outside of the ring and some of the fingers should point to the inside of the ring.

2. Curl and scrunch the fingers to give the wreath a three-dimensional appearance.

3. Add a large bow and a greeting, if appropriate.

Menorah

The Festival of Lights, which is celebrated by the Jewish people, is called Hanukkah. It is an eight-day celebration that begins by lighting a special menorah called a *hanukiyah*. This special menorah has nine candles. One candle, the *shamash*, is used to light one of the other eight each evening.

Materials

- dark blue or silver/gray tempera paint
- light blue or white and yellow construction paper
- glitter, jewels, sequins, etc.
- cookie sheet with sides
- markers
- newspaper
- hand soap, water, and towels
- painting smocks

Preparation

1. Prepare an area for painting and establish a cleanup area close by.
2. Pour a thin layer of paint in the cookie sheet and place the tray on newspaper.
3. Prepare your candle and flame cutouts.
4. Talk about the significance of a menorah. Ask students to share ways in which candles factor into their family traditions.

Procedure

1. Have students hold their hands up in the air. Ask them to join their hands in front of them, pressing their thumbs together. Explain that they are going to create menorah prints using their hands. The thumbs will create the central candle holder. The fingers will be the remaining eight candles. Later, they will add the shamash and flames.

3. Have students take turns dipping their hands in the paint and pressing them on the paper as practiced. Remind them to keep their thumbs together or to overlap them.

4. Once the paint has dried, students can decorate the menorahs with glitter, jewels, etc.

5. Add shamash candles and flames to the menorah.

Display Suggestion

Post the completed work around the room where students can reach them. Each day of Hanukkah have students "light" a new flame on the Hanukkah menorah or hanukiyah.

Candle and Flame Patterns

Reindeer

Materials

- dark brown construction paper
- light brown construction paper
- crayons or colored markers
- eyes, nose, and mouth patterns (see below)
- white, black, and red construction paper
- glue
- scissors
- pencils

Procedure

1. Help each student trace his or her shoe outline on a piece of light brown construction paper, or have students work in pairs and help each other trace their shoes.

2. Let students cut out their traced shoe shapes. Explain that these shapes will become the reindeers' heads. It is up to each student to decide if the wider part of the shoeprint should be the top of the head or the bottom.

3. Have each student fold a piece of darker brown construction paper in half and trace his or her handprint on the paper.

4. Cut out the handprint so these will be the antlers. Have each student glue a set of antlers to the top of his or her reindeer's head.

5. Let students color the facial features of their reindeer, or use the patterns below to provide them with precut eyes, noses, and mouths to glue onto the reindeer.

6. Have students cut ears from brown paper if they wish to add them.

Display Suggestions

- Cut a small hole in each reindeer head where the nose would be. Hang a string of red lights across a wall. Put a reindeer head over each red light. The paper should be around the light holder, not the red light itself. When the red lights are turned on, a string of red-nosed reindeer will greet you.
- Attach each reindeer head to a headband to be worn.

Eyes, Nose, and Mouth Patterns

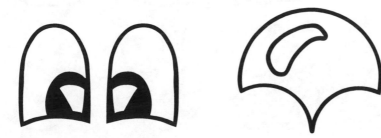

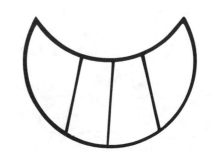

Gloves and Mittens

Materials

- colored construction paper
- assorted decorative materials such as yarn, ribbon, sequins, glitter, stickers, and buttons
- collection of mittens and gloves
- glue and/or glue sticks

Procedure

1. Share a collection of gloves and mittens with students. Talk about the differences and similarities. Take a poll and see who prefers mittens and who prefers gloves. Make a chart or graph.

2. Ask students to spread their fingers and trace their hands on colored construction paper if they wish to make gloves. If they wish to make mittens, have them trace their hands with their fingers touching, just as they would be if they were wearing mittens.

3. Provide scissors so the completed tracings can be cut out.

4. Decorate the gloves and mittens. If appropriate, encourage students to create matching pairs of gloves or mittens.

Display Suggestions

- Line up all the pairs of mittens and use them to practice counting by twos or skip counting. Use the pairs of gloves to count by fives or tens.

- The gloves and mittens could be used to highlight student work on a winter board. Simply place the mittens or gloves on the upper left and right corners of student work pages as if they were holding up the pages.

- Have students trace their hands on a sheet of paper. Attach the gloves or mittens over the hands with brads.

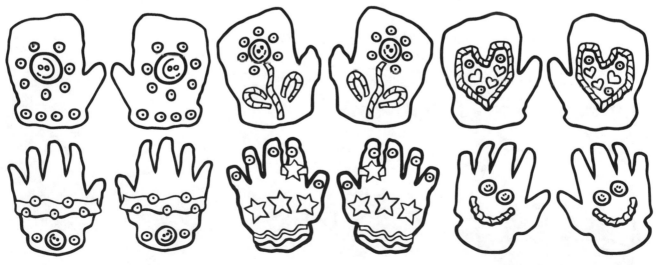

Thumbprint Animals

Materials

- Thumbprint Patterns (page 36)
- Thumbprint Animal Cards (page 37)
- magnifying glasses
- washable ink stamp pads

- paper
- fine-tip black markers
- crayons or colored markers
- wipes or soap and water

Preparation

1. Make copies of the Thumbprint Patterns and the Thumbprint Animal Cards. Enlarge them if possible.

2. Prepare an area for students to clean their hands after printing.

Procedure

1. Show students how to press their thumbs or index fingers into the stamp pads and then press them onto the paper to make fingerprints.

2. Spend some time practicing fingerprinting. If time allows, examine and compare the fingerprints using magnifying glasses. Encourage students to compare fingerprints and guide them to the discovery that no two people have the same prints.

3. Ask students to create different animals out of their prints. If some guidance is needed, you can demonstrate how to make different types of animals by adding details. Use the enlarged thumbprint patterns provided. Start by using the print as a body and add legs, a head, and a tail. Add details to create a cat, dog, or other animal. Keep the illustrations simple and assure students that there is not a right way to do it.

4. After extended practice, have students make thumbprints on clean pieces of paper. Ask them to leave space between the prints so details can be added.

5. Use the black markers to add details to make the thumbprints look like animals. Foster creativity. Encourage students to try different things and share their creations. See who will be the first to connect a string of prints to make a snake or an insect or come up with a new animal.

6. Use the crayons or colored markers to create scenery and other details.

Display Suggestions

- Display student work with the title "Thumbprint Art." Leave stamp pads and magnifying glasses available in the writing or art area and encourage students to keep adding to the display as new ideas come to them.

- Compile the art in a class book. Help students label their work or write stories about their thumbprint pictures.

Thumbprint Patterns

Thumbprint Animal Cards

ant

cat

bee

spider

snake

caterpillar

"I Love You"

Teach students how to say, "I love you" in sign language. Explain that sign language is another way to communicate. In sign language, hand movements are used in place of words. The following hand signs say "I love you."

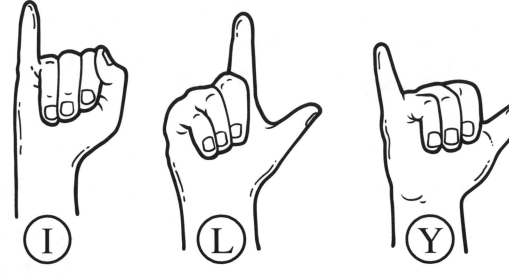

Materials

- pencils
- safety scissors
- red construction paper
- pink construction paper
- glue sticks
- small, red heart stickers

Procedure

1. Ask students to trace their hands on pink or red pieces of construction paper.

2. Provide scissors to cut out the tracings.

3. Model how to fold the two middle fingers down toward the palm. Extend the thumb to form an "L" shape. Explain that this hand sign combines the three individual signs. It, too, means "I love you."

4. Give each student a heart sticker to place in the palm of the cut-out hand.

Display Suggestion

- Attach the "I Love You" hand shapes to a bulletin board in the shape of a heart. Ask each student to tell you where to attach his or her hand to complete the heart shape.

38

A New Kind of Heart

Students will be creating decorative hearts using the sides of their curved hands to create patterns on heart-shaped paper.

Materials

- red, pink, and white tempera paint
- red, pink, and white construction paper
- glitter
- sturdy paper plates or cookie sheets with edges

- red, white, pink, and purple crayons
- hand soap, water, and towels
- old shirts or smocks
- heart pattern (page 40)

Alternative: You may wish to encourage students to experiment with red and white paint to make their own shade of pink.

Preparation

1. Use the heart pattern to create heart templates on cardboard or tagboard.

2. Precut red, pink, and white heart shapes or encourage students to trace and cut their own hearts using the heart templates.

3. Prepare for a messy activity. Arrange newspaper under plates of paint. Pour a thin layer of paint onto the plates or trays.

4. Establish a clean up area.

Procedure

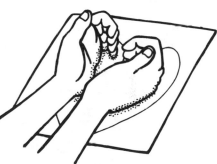

1. Model how to hold hands to create a heart pattern on construction paper. Hold hands out and curve fingers. Ask students to hold their hands like this and adjust their fingers until they can see a heart shape. The hands do not need to touch each other to create the suggestion of the shape. Explain that it may not be perfect, but should be heart-like. The bigger the hand, the easier it is to see! Some students may find it is easier to see the heart if they hold their hands a bit farther apart.

2. Have students choose a paint color and a paper color. Label the back of the heart paper chosen.

3. Take turns dipping curved hands into the paint (pinkie-side down) and pressing it on paper.

4. Sprinkle the handprint hearts with glitter and let the handprints dry.

Display Suggestions

- Mount the handprint hearts on larger hearts and have students decorate them. Display them around the classroom.
- Use the hearts to make cards for Valentine's Day.

Heart Pattern

In Like a Lion

"If March comes in like a lion, it will go out like a lamb." Share this old saying and other weather-related sayings with students while working on the project. Consider writing a collection of sayings on chart paper and adding to it during the month.

Materials

- yellow construction paper
- lion face pattern (page 42)
- tan and light brown crayons
- safety scissors
- pencils

Procedure

1. Ask students to trace their hands on pieces of yellow construction paper.

2. When students have finished tracing their hands, provide scissors for them to cut out the tracings.

3. Explain to students that the hands will be used to create the lion's mane on their display. Ask students to add tan and brown lines to the hands to suggest the hair/fur on a male lion's head.

Lion Head Assembly

1. Enlarge the lion face pattern to fit the display area or bulletin board. Use yellow paper for the face and color the eyes black.

2. Arrange the completed hand shapes around the lion's face to represent the lion's mane.

3. Curl or round the fingers on the hands to add dimension.

Display Suggestions

- Use the completed Lion as a door decoration.

- Use the Lion in conjunction with the Lamb and Wind patterns to create a display with the phrase "…if March comes in like a lion, it will go out like a lamb..." on a banner or board (See page 43.).

- Use the Lion face and the Lamb to create a graph. See if there are more lion or lamb days in the week or month.

Lion Face

Lamb

Materials

- Lamb Face, Hooves, and Tail (page 44)
- white paper plates
- cotton balls
- glue

Procedure

1. Glue the lamb's face, hooves, and tail onto a white paper plate.

2. Ask students to pull apart cotton balls and glue them to the lamb's body and around the face. Try not to cover the features.

Display Suggestion

Use the lamb with the wind pattern (page 45) and the lion head to decorate a spring bulletin board.

If March comes in like a lion, it will go out like a lamb

Lamb Face, Hooves, and Tail

Wind

Shamrocks

Materials

- shamrock patterns (page 47)
- light and dark green tempera paint
- light and dark green construction paper
- 3 cookie sheets with sides
- hand soap, water and towels
- newspaper
- gold glitter
- safety scissors
- glue or a stapler

Preparation

1. Prepare an area for painting and establish a cleanup area close by.

2. Place the two trays on newspaper. Pour a thin layer of each color green in a different cookie tray. This will be the Paint Station.

3. Use the third cookie tray for a Glitter Station. Place the container of glitter in the tray.

4. Make copies of the shamrock patterns for each student on different colors of green paper. Assemble one for demonstration purposes.

Procedure

1. Have students choose the paper color they prefer and have them cut out the four pieces.

2. Assemble the shamrock by stapling or gluing the leaflets to the stem.

3. Demonstrate to students how to hold their hands in fists, thumbs up, and dip their hands into the tray of green paint and then onto the shamrock to create a print. Have them practice on a table or desk, explaining that a fist print should fit into each of the leaflets of the shamrock.

4. Have each student take his or her completed shamrock to the Paint Station and choose the color green they wish to use to decorate their shamrock.

5. Make three fist prints, one on each leaflet and proceed to the Glitter Station while the paint is still wet.

6. Place the painted shamrock on the tray in the Glitter Station and sprinkle glitter on the wet paint. Shake off the extra glitter into the tray and set the shamrock aside to dry.

Shamrock Patterns

Spring Flowers

Materials

- green, white, and pastel-colored construction paper
- multi-colored paper cupcake liners
- Leaves and Stems patterns (page 49)
- pencils
- safety scissors

Procedure for Tulip Flowers

1. Have students place their hands, with the fingers open but thumb close to the side of the hand, on pastel pieces of construction paper. Ask students to trace around their hands with a pencil.

2. When the students have finished tracing their hands, provide scissors for them to cut out their tracings. Encourage them to round the base of the flower (palm of the hand) to create a tulip-like shape.

3. Add leaves and stems to complete the flowers.

Procedure for Daisy Flower

1. Have students use pencils to trace their hands with fingers spread apart on white construction paper.

2. When the students have finished tracing their hands, provide scissors for them to cut them out.

3. Have four or five students combine their handprints (at the palms) and attach them to the back of a cupcake liner to create a flower.

4. Add leaves and stems to complete the flowers.

Display Suggestion

Cover a display area or bulletin board to create a spring outdoor scene.

1. Use blue paper at the top for sky. Add white, fluffy clouds and a sun.

2. Use green paper at the bottom for grass. Snip the edge of the green paper to give the suggestion of individual blades.

3. Add the "flowers" to create a spring garden. Encourage students to choose where to put their flowers. Ask them to use directional words like *above*, *below*, and *beside*.

Leaves and Stems

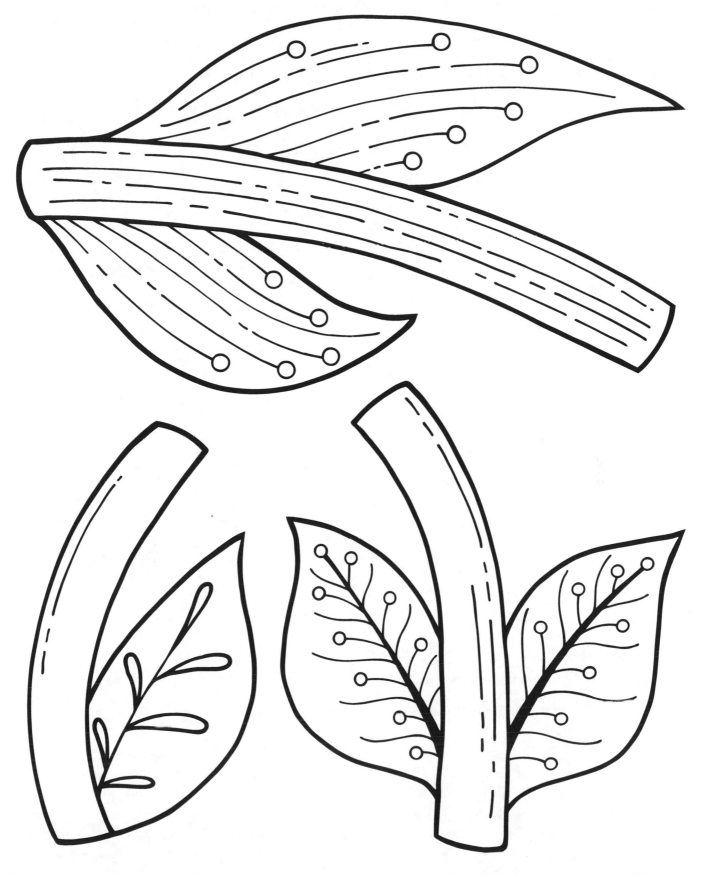

Ducks

Materials

- copies of Duck Patterns and Song (page 51)
- white and orange construction paper
- blue construction paper
- white feathers or white tissue paper
- large wiggly eyes
- pencils and markers
- glue
- safety scissors

Preparation

1. Copy the beak and feet patterns onto orange paper or have students color them.

2. Arrange an area for students to glue feathers to ducks.

3. Copy the lilypads onto green paper or have students color them.

Procedure

1. Have each student trace one shoe print and two handprints on the white paper and cut them out. When necessary, help them with tracing and cutting.

2. Have students arrange the three white patterns so that the footprint will be the body of the bird. Glue the wings (handprints) to either side in the middle of the foot (instep).

4. Glue white feathers or shredded white tissue paper to the duck and put the patterns aside until dry.

5. Fold the beaks and glue the back of one side to the duck's head.

6. Add wiggly eyes and two webbed feet to complete the duck.

7. Glue the completed duck, lilypad, and song onto blue paper.

Display Suggestions

- Teach students the song, *Little White Duck*, and have them sing the song while holding their completed duck pages. Display the work on a bulletin board or add them to student portfolios.

- Make one larger duck (teacher's foot and handprints) using white paper for the head, body, and wings. Students will make ducklings using their footprints and yellow paper. Create a pond scene bulletin board display with the white duck surrounded by smaller yellow ducklings.

Duck Patterns and Song

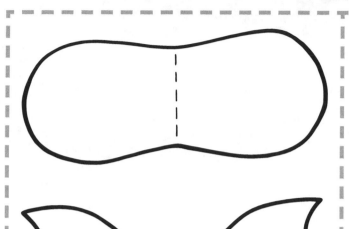

Little White Duck

There's a little white duck
Sitting in the water.
A little white duck
Doing what he ought to.
He took a bite of a lily pad,
Flapped his wings and he said,
"I'm glad I'm a little white duck,
Sitting in the water."
Quack, Quack, Quack.

Little White Duck

There's a little white duck
Sitting in the water.
A little white duck
Doing what he ought to.
He took a bite of a lily pad,
Flapped his wings and he said,
"I'm glad I'm a little white duck,
Sitting in the water."
Quack, Quack, Quack.

Rabbits

Materials

- Rabbit face pattern (page 53)
- light brown, tan, or white construction paper
- pink, blue, yellow, and lavender construction paper
- pom poms

- safety scissors
- pencils
- markers or crayons
- *optional*: thin strips of black paper or chenille sticks for whiskers

Preparation

1. Use the outer oval on the rabbit face pattern as a guide to cut the pastel-colored paper for the head Make one for each student.

2. Copy the rabbit face pattern (inner oval) onto light brown, tan, or white construction paper for each student. **Note:** Two face patterns will fit on a page when copying.

3. Cut the face patterns out and make copies for each student.

Procedure

1. Hand out a face pattern to each student and have them choose a piece of construction paper to make ears. Explain that they can choose any color they want, and it does not have to match the face color. Not all rabbits are alike!

2. Instruct students to fold their choice of colored construction paper in half and trace and cut out two shoeprints.

3. Have students choose a colored oval (rabbit head) and attach the rabbit faces.

4. Glue shoeprints (ears) to the back of the rabbit head.

5. Draw or add whiskers and a pom pom nose.

Display Suggestions

- Cut out eye holes and make rabbit masks. Have students hop around the classroom or have a parade outdoors while wearing their rabbit masks.

- Add the rabbits to large pieces of folded construction paper. Create Easter cards for students to share with family and friends.

- Attach the finished projects to headbands to be worn during a spring or Easter celebration.

Rabbit Face

Directions: Use the outer oval as a guide to cut the colored construction paper.

Butterfly Cards

Materials

- construction paper—pastel colors
- chenille sticks (black or brown)
- glue sticks
- pencils
- safety scissors
- felt pens

Procedure

1. Chose two different colored pieces of paper, one for the card and the other for the butterfly.

2. Have students trace their hands, keeping their fingers close together, on a folded piece of construction paper.

Note: If cutting through two pieces of paper is too difficult, have students trace their hands twice. Remind students to keep the hand that is on the paper still and use the other hand to move the pencil. For some students, it helps to put a little piece of rolled-up tape on the underside of the construction paper while tracing to keep the paper from moving.

3. When students have finished tracing their hands, have them cut out the tracings. They should have two hand shapes when they are finished.

4. Fold the second piece of paper in half like a card. Glue the two shapes on the front of the card with the thumb sides over-lapping to make a butterfly.

5. Have the students cut the construction paper scraps into shapes to glue on the butterfly wings for decoration. Add chenille stick antennae.

Display Suggestions

- Encourage each student to write a message to a parent, sibling, or friend inside his or her card. If necessary, have students dictate a message while you write it in the card. Encourage each student to write his or her name at the end of the message.
- Create a set of cards to be used as class "Thank You" cards. Create a template for the words "Thank You" that students can add to their cards.

Animals in the Wild

Elephant

Materials

- pictures or books about elephants in the wild
- gray tempera paint (or black and white)
- paintbrushes and small cups
- white or tan paper
- cookie sheets with sides
- hand soap, water, and towels
- newspaper
- wiggly eyes
- felt pens
- safety scissors

Preparation

1. Prepare an area for painting and establish a cleanup area close by.

2. Pour a thin layer of gray paint in a cookie tray. Add small cups of gray paint and paintbrushes. Place the tray and cups on newspaper. This will bc the Paint Station. If time allows, let students create different shades of gray by mixing black and white paint.

Procedure

1. Share pictures and stories of elephants with students. Discuss the elephant's body type and characteristics. Mention the trunk, tusks, large ears, small tail, and four legs. Explain that elephants have five toes but that we cannot really see them, just the nails. Note the animal's color. Ask students if they know what two colors mixed together will create gray? *(black and white)*

2. Explain to students that they will be laying their hands flat, palm-side down with thumbs pointing out, into gray paint and then pressing them onto paper to make elephants. Their palms will form the back of the elephant, their fingers the legs, and their thumbs the trunks.

3. After the palm prints have been made, have students wash their hands. Then ask students to observe their prints with the fingers facing down. Ask each student to use a paintbrush to paint a tail on the side opposite the trunk and then set the print aside to dry.

4. When dry, details can be added to the print. Ask students to draw facial features, ears, toes, and other details. Add wiggly eyes and tusks cut from paper and then cut out the finished prints.

Display Suggestions

- Create a bulletin board featuring wildlife in Africa. Incorporate some or all of the animals featured on pages 55–57. Start with a light blue background. Use tissue paper, crepe paper, and construction paper to add a river, grasses, and trees to the scene.

- Create grassland or forest scenes on light blue construction paper. Have children draw or cut out trees, ground cover, and other items. Add the elephants and text, if appropriate.

- If more than one type of wild animal handprint is done, create a book and title it *Animals in the Wild*. Perhaps students will come up with additional animals to add to the project.

Animals in the Wild *(cont.)*

Giraffe

Materials

- pictures or books about giraffes in the wild
- light brown construction paper
- brown pom poms
- yellow and brown tempera paint
- wiggly eyes
- paintbrushes and small cups
- cookie sheet with sides
- hand soap, water and towels
- newspaper
- glue

Preparation

1. Prepare an area for painting and establish a cleanup area close by.

2. Pour a thin layer of yellow paint in a cookie tray. Add small cups of brown paint and paintbrushes. Place the tray and cups on newspaper. This will be the Paint Station.

Procedure

1. Share pictures and books about giraffes with students. Talk about the giraffe's body type, coloring, and distinguishing characteristics. No two giraffes have the same pattern of brown spots. Mention that giraffes are the tallest of all land-living mammals and that they have blue-black tongues! Giraffes also have two to four blunt horns on the tops of their heads.

2. Instruct students to roll up their sleeves for this print since they will be using their hands and their arms to the elbows. Practice holding hands with the tips of the four fingers joined and touching the thumb. This will form the giraffe's face.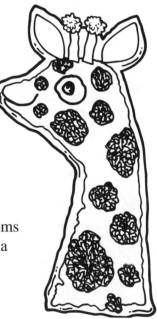

3. Have each student place his or her arm and hand in the yellow paint. Make a print on light brown construction paper and wash hands and arms.

4. Then, students may go back to the paint station and add brown spots to their prints to create unique patterns.

5. They should finish the activity by adding eyes and horns. Pom poms can also be added to the tops of the horns if students wish to have a female giraffe. Males tend to have horns with tufts worn down.

6. Cut out the finished giraffes when dry.

Display

- Create a bulletin board featuring wildlife in Africa. Add acacia trees, and place the giraffe heads so they appear to be popping through the branches. See page 55 for additional ideas.
- Create a scene on light blue construction paper. Have children draw or cut out trees, ground cover, and other items. Add the cut-out giraffes and text, if appropriate.

Animals in the Wild *(cont.)*

Crocodile

Materials

- pictures or books about crocodiles in the wild
- gray construction paper
- dark green, light green, and gray tempera paint
- white paper
- paintbrushes and cups
- hand soap, water, and towels
- newspaper
- scissors, glue, and pencils

Preparation

1. Prepare an area for painting and establish a cleanup area close by.

2. Fill small cups with green and gray paint. Place the cups and paintbrushes on newspaper. This will be the Paint Station.

Procedure

1. Share pictures and books about crocodiles with students. Talk about the crocodiles' appearance. Mention that they are grayish green and have sharp claws and one of the strongest bites of any animal. They eat fish, frogs, reptiles, and small animals.

2. Explain to students that they will create the head of their crocodiles using their hands and then draw the animals' bodies. Have students hold up their hands and imagine that their thumbs are the lower jaw of the crocodile and their fingers are the upper jaw. Clamp the fingers together repeatedly to simulate the jaws opening and closing.

3. Have students lay their hands down on one end of the large sheet of construction paper. The elbow should be in the middle of the page. The fingers will form the head and upper jaw. The thumb will be the lower jaw. Remind students to hold their hands so that the crocodile's mouth appears open.

4. Have students trace the outlines of their hands and arms. Then, ask them to remove their hands and finish the drawings by adding long tails and legs with claws.

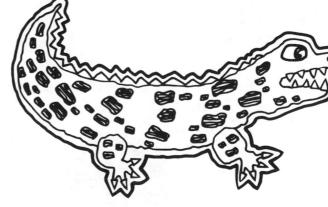

5. Next, have them cut out teeth and glue them in place or draw them in the open mouths.

6. Finally, have students paint the completed pictures using gray and green paint.

7. Let them dry, then cut out the completed versions.

Display Suggestions

- Create a bulletin board featuring a wide river in Africa. Create rocks, trees and other items to enhance the scene using paper and other materials. Arrange the cut-out crocodiles in and near the water. Add text, if appropriate. See page 55 for additional ideas.

- If more than one wild animal handprint is done, create a book and title it *Animals in the Wild.* Perhaps students will come up with additional animals to add to the project.

Sun

This group project can make a wonderful door display or room decoration or enhance a spring/summer bulletin board.

Materials

- shades of yellow and/or pale orange construction paper
- Sun Face pattern (page 59)
- pencils
- safety scissors
- tape or glue

Preparation

1. Enlarge the Sun Face pattern and copy it onto yellow paper.

Procedure

1. Ask students to trace their hands on yellow and pale orange construction paper. Explain that they will use them to create the rays of the sun.

2. When students have finished tracing their hands, provide scissors for them to cut out their tracings.

3. Place the sun face down on a table and have students attach their hands to the rim. Have them put the tape or glue on the palm end of the handprint so the fingers will fan out.

4. Flip the assemblage over and add more hands if needed to create a bright, glowing sun.

Display Suggestions

- Use the completed sun as a door decoration or welcome sign.
- Add the sun to a bulletin board display.

Sun Face

Fish

Materials

- assorted colors of construction paper
- materials to decorate fish—glitter, sequins, and foil pieces
- glue sticks
- pencils
- safety scissors

Procedure

1. Ask students to trace their hands on their choices of construction paper. Have them hold their fingers tightly together and extend their thumbs to make a fin shape.

2. When students have finished tracing their hands, provide scissors for them to cut out the tracings.

3. Make available an assortment of materials so students can decorate the fish they made. Make sure to add an eye and a fin.

Display Suggestions

- Use the fishbowl pattern on page 61. Have each student create fish for his or her fishbowl. Write stories about the fish.

- Create an ocean backdrop on a bulletin board or display area. Use the students' fish to create an underwater scene.

  1. Use medium or dark blue paper for the water.

  2. Add green, red, and brown seaweed and brown or sand-colored paper to create the ocean floor.

  3. Have students choose where they would like their fish to be placed. Do they want to be part of a school or swimming by themselves?

Fish Bowl

Sparkling Fireworks

Materials

- white construction paper
- colored glitter and sparkling confetti
- metallic chenille sticks
- cookie sheet or tray with sides
- safety scissors
- vase, coffee can, or tall container
- glue or tape
- pencils

Procedure

1. Ask students to trace their hands on pieces of white construction paper.

2. When students have finished tracing their hands, provide scissors for them to cut out the hand tracings.

3. Ask students to put glue on the hand shape and carefully lay it in the tray. Sprinkle glitter on the glue.

4. Shake the excess glitter off the glittery handprint and onto the tray. Let the print dry.

5. Once dry, tape or glue a metallic chenille stick to the back of the sparkly hand.

Display Suggestion

Combine the hands to create a sparkling display, similar to fireworks. Arrange the hands in a vase. Bend the chenille sticks, allowing them to fan out over the top of the container. If appropriate, decorate the container with stars. Patterns are provided below.

Star Patterns

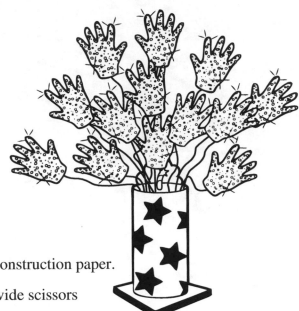

Eagle

The bald eagle is the national bird of the United States. It is a raptor with dark brown feathers on its body and white head and tail feathers. It tends to live near rivers and lakes and mainly eats fish but can eat other animals as well. Its strong wings and tail allow it to soar in the sky searching for prey.

Materials

- eagle body pattern (page 64)
- pictures and books featuring bald eagles
- brown construction paper
- black, brown, and yellow crayons
- safety scissors
- pencils
- glue

Preparation

1. Make copies of the eagle body for each student.

2. Create a display of books and pictures of bald eagles.

Procedure

1. Share pictures and information about bald eagles with students.

2. Provide each student with an eagle body pattern. Have them color the body brown or a mixture of brown and black. Color the beak and talons yellow. Leave the head and tail feathers white.

3. Have each student fold his or her piece of brown construction paper in half.

4. Have them trace their hands with fingers separated on the paper. Explain that they will make the eagle's wings with their handprints.

3. Glue the hands (wings) to the back of the eagle's body.

Display Suggestions

- Hang flying eagles from the ceiling on yarn or ropes strung across the classroom.
- Incorporate the eagles into a patriotic display or 4th of July bulletin board.

Eagle Body